Quick and Easy COOKBOOK

Written by Robyn Supraner
Illustrated by Renzo Barto

Troll Associates

Library of Congress Cataloging in Publication Data

Supraner, Robyn.
   Quick and easy cookbook.

   SUMMARY: Includes 21 easy-to-make recipes for
such dishes as homemade applesauce, egg salad,
hamburger heroes, tossed green salad, fruity fruit
punch, dandy candy chews, carrot slaw, and frozen
bananas.
   1. Cookery—Juvenile literature.   [1. Cookery]
I. Barto, Renzo.   II. Title.
TX652.5.S94   641.5´123   80-24021
ISBN 0-89375-438-2 (Case)
ISBN 0-89375-439-0 (p.bk.)

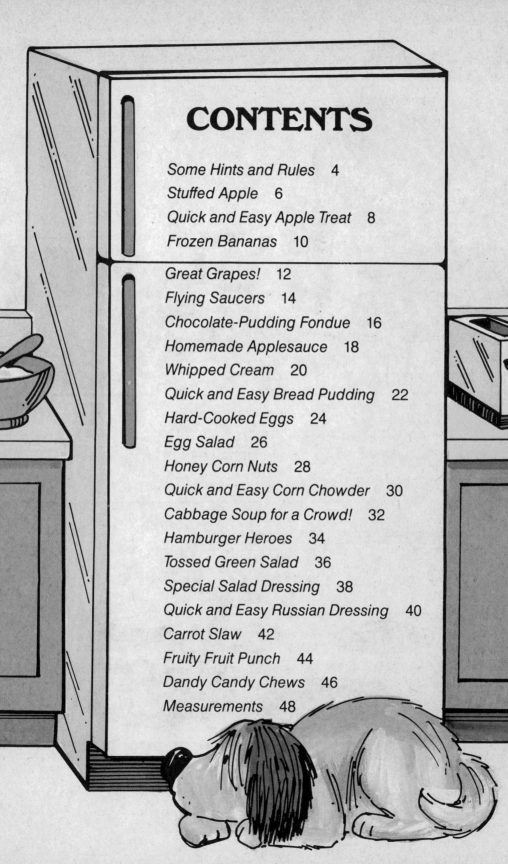

CONTENTS

SOME HINTS AND RULES:

1 Read the whole recipe before you begin. Have your ingredients and utensils ready before you start to cook.

2 Always ask for permission to use the oven, the broiler, or the stove. Ask a grownup for help in setting the oven temperature.

3 When you are working at the stove, turn all pot handles away from you.

4 Never use a wet potholder! It won't protect you from the heat.

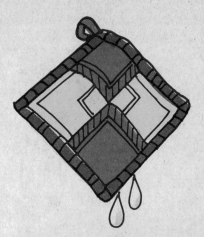

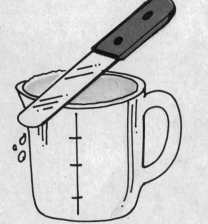

5 For exact measurements, level dry ingredients with the flat side of a butter knife.

6 Don't worry if things don't come out right the first time. So what? Try again! Enjoy yourself. Taste and smell the food. Cooking is fun!

STUFFED APPLE

Here's what you need:

Apple corer

Knife

Spoon

Plate

1 Beautiful apple

GOOEY PEANUT BUTTER

Your favorite peanut butter

Here's what you do:

1 Wash and dry the apple. Polish it until it shines.

2 With the corer, carefully remove the core and seeds from the center of the apple.

 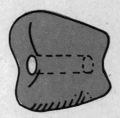

3 Using a spoon, stuff the apple with peanut butter.

4 Lay the apple on its side, and cut it into 4 or 5 slices.

5 Arrange the slices on a pretty plate.

6 Eat!

Hint: Stuffed apples taste especially good with lots of ice-cold milk. Also, try mixing a few raisins into the peanut butter before stuffing the apple.

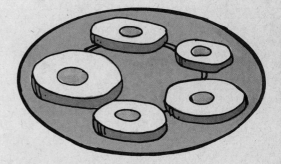

QUICK AND EASY APPLE TREAT

Here's what you need:

Measuring cup

Can opener

Cinnamon

Raisins

Chopped walnuts

Bowl

Wooden spoon

1 Jar applesauce

½ Cup pineapple

Here's what you do:

1 Combine the applesauce, pineapple, some raisins, a few walnuts, and a bit of cinnamon in a mixing bowl.

2 Stir, gently, with a wooden spoon.

3 Chill the mixture in the refrigerator for at least 4 hours.
   Yield: 4–6 servings.

Enjoy this dish plain or topped with whipped cream. How about adding some vanilla ice cream? Or try it topped with yogurt and a handful of granola!

FROZEN BANANAS

Here's what you need:

4 Ripe bananas

Cinnamon

Nutmeg

Honey

Granola

Chopped peanuts

Aluminum foil

Pastry brush

Here's what you do:

1   Peel the bananas. Place each one on a sheet of aluminum foil.

2   Sprinkle one banana with cinnamon.

3   Sprinkle one with nutmeg.

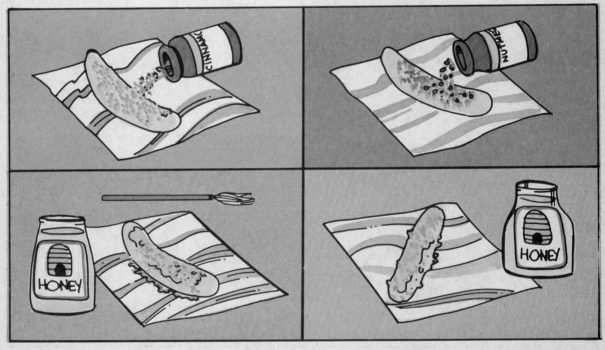

4   Brush one with honey and roll it in granola.

5   Brush one with honey and roll it in chopped peanuts.

6   Wrap the foil around each banana.

7   Put the bananas in the freezer, and freeze them for 24 hours.

Unwrap one banana, a little at a time, and eat it as you would a popsicle. This recipe is enough for one person for four days or four people for one day. If you are going to share them, make sure that everyone has a taste of each kind of banana. Try other combinations. A plain frozen banana is delicious, too!

GREAT GRAPES!

Here's what you need:

Tablespoon

Measuring cup

Cereal bowl

Brown sugar

½ Cup yogurt or sour cream

1 Cup green seedless grapes

Here's what you do:

1 Combine the grapes, yogurt or sour cream, and a sprinkling of brown sugar in the cereal bowl.

2 Stir with your tablespoon and eat.

Hint: This recipe is also delicious when made with fresh, sliced peaches instead of grapes.

FLYING SAUCERS

Here's what you need:

Spoon

Butter knife

Small bowl

6–8 Squares of aluminum foil

½ Pint chocolate-mint ice cream

12–16 Large chocolate cookies

Here's what you do:

1 Empty the ice cream into a bowl.

2 With a spoon, stir the ice cream until it softens just a little.

3 With a butter knife, spread the softened ice cream on a cookie. Cover it, quickly, with another cookie.

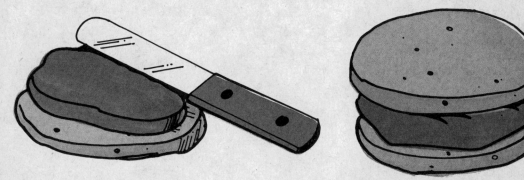

4 Wrap the ice-cream sandwich in a square of aluminum foil, and pop it into the freezer.

5 Make 5–7 more sandwiches the same way. How many sandwiches you get depends on how big the cookies are and how much ice cream you use. *Remember to work quickly.* Ice-cream soup makes sloppy sandwiches!

6 Freeze the sandwiches for at least 24 hours.

Yield: 6–8 Flying Saucers

Hint: Try other combinations. How about pistachio ice cream and almond cookies, or peanut-butter cookies with vanilla ice cream?

CHOCOLATE-PUDDING FONDUE

Note: This recipe calls for use of the stove. If you are not allowed to use the stove by yourself, ask a grownup for help.

Here's what you need:

Wooden spoon

4 Plates

Napkins

4 Knives

Measuring cup

4 Fondue forks

Medium-size pot with a handle   Clean dishtowel   Potholder

1 Box chocolate pudding mix (not "instant")

Shredded coconut

2 Cups milk

4 Firm bananas

Here's what you do:

1 This fondue makes enough for four people, so set four places at the table. Set out plates, knives, forks, and napkins.

2 Put a dishtowel in the center of the table.

3 Following the directions on the box, make the chocolate pudding, using 2 cups of milk.

Hint: Add just a little of the milk to the powdered pudding, at first. Then stir out all the lumps and bumps with a wooden spoon. When the pudding is smooth, add the rest of the milk, stirring all the time.

4 Using a potholder, carry the pot of hot pudding to the table, and place it on the dishtowel.

5 Peel the bananas, and put one on each plate. Put a bowl of shredded coconut on the table.

To eat:

1 Cut your banana into bite-size chunks.

2 Spear a banana chunk with your fork, and dip it into the hot pudding. Then, dip it into the coconut.

3 Repeat, until every gooey bit is gone!

4 Use the napkins to catch the drips.

HOMEMADE APPLESAUCE

Note: This recipe calls for use of a knife and the stove. Ask a grownup for help, if you are not allowed to use these items by yourself.

Here's what you need:

Measuring cup

Knife

Vegetable scraper

Wooden spoon

4 Apples

Pot with a cover

Potholder

⅓ Cup water

¼ Cup sugar or honey

Here's what you do:

1   Wash the apples.

2   Cut each apple into quarters.

3   Cut out the apple cores and seeds.

4   Peel the apple pieces with a vegetable scraper.

5   Put the apples and water into the pot. Set them on the stove over a low heat.

6   Cover the pot and cook the apples, very gently, for about 15 minutes or until they are soft. Stir them with the wooden spoon from time to time. Add a bit more water, if you think they are burning. *Remember! The pot is hot! Use your potholder!*

7   While the applesauce is hot, add the honey or sugar. Stir until the sugar melts or the honey is well blended.

8   Mash the applesauce with a wooden spoon until it is smooth. Leave some lumps in it, if you like it chunky.

9   Serve the applesauce while it is warm, or chill it in the refrigerator.

WHIPPED CREAM

Note: Check first, with an adult, if you plan to use an electric beater for this recipe.

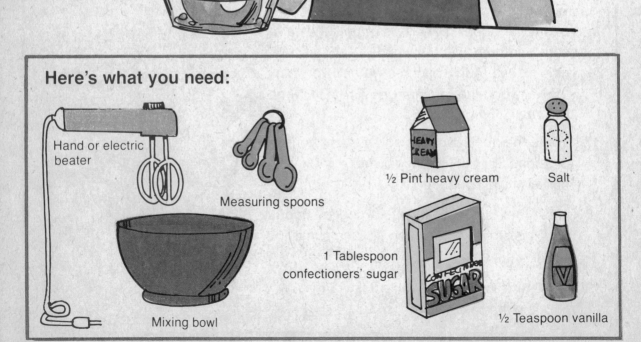

Here's what you need:

Hand or electric beater

Measuring spoons

½ Pint heavy cream

Salt

Mixing bowl

1 Tablespoon confectioners' sugar

½ Teaspoon vanilla

Here's what you do:

1   Chill the cream, the bowl, and the beaters in the freezer for 15 minutes.

2   Pour the cream into the bowl.

3   With the beater, whip the cream until it starts to thicken.

4   Add a pinch of salt, the vanilla, and the confectioners' sugar.

5   Continue beating, until the cream is thick enough to stand up in firm peaks. (Don't beat it too long, or you will wind up with a bowl of butter!)

6   Store the whipped cream in the refrigerator until you are ready to use it.

Whipped cream tastes delicious on pies and puddings. Add a tablespoon or two of sweetened cocoa instead of the confectioners' sugar. Presto! *Chocolate whipped cream!*

QUICK AND EASY BREAD PUDDING

Note: This recipe calls for use of the oven. If you are not allowed to use the oven by yourself, ask an adult for help.

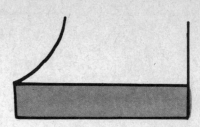

Here's what you need:

Fork

Measuring spoons

Small baking dish

Potholders

White bread

Vanilla

Cinnamon

Honey or sugar

Egg

Milk

Here's what you do:

1. Set the oven for 350°.

2. Break one egg into a baking dish. Beat it with a fork until it is bubbly.

3. Add 2 teaspoons of honey or sugar and ½ teaspoon vanilla. Beat some more.

4. Add 6 ounces of milk, slowly. Continue to beat the mixture with a fork until everything is well blended.

5. Break the slice of bread into about 8 small pieces. Press them into the egg mixture with your fork. Let them soak for a minute or two, pressing with your fork to make sure they are covered.

6. Sprinkle the mixture lightly, with cinnamon.

7. Put the pudding, *very carefully,* on the middle shelf of the oven, and close the oven door. *Remember to use potholders!*

8. Bake the pudding for 25–30 minutes, until it puffs up and is golden brown on top.

9. Using potholders, remove the finished pudding from the oven and let it cool a bit.

10. Eat and enjoy!

HARD-COOKED EGGS

Note: If you are not allowed to use the stove by yourself, ask a grownup for help.

Here's what you need:

Pot

Potholder

4 Eggs

Here's what you do:

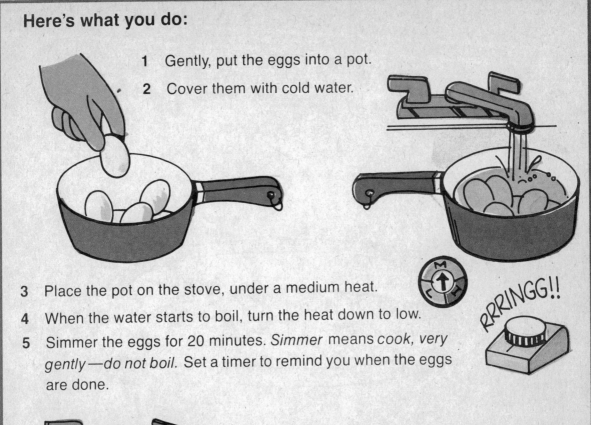

1 Gently, put the eggs into a pot.

2 Cover them with cold water.

3 Place the pot on the stove, under a medium heat.

4 When the water starts to boil, turn the heat down to low.

5 Simmer the eggs for 20 minutes. *Simmer* means *cook, very gently—do not boil.* Set a timer to remind you when the eggs are done.

RRRINGG!!

6 As soon as they are ready, place the eggs under cold, running water. Pot handles can get hot! Remember to use a potholder.

7 Turn off the faucet, and chill the eggs.

8 When the eggs are chilled, remove their shells. (*Hint:* Eggshells are easier to remove when you start at the wide end of the egg.)

What can you do with hard-cooked eggs? Why, make egg salad, of course, or deviled eggs. Better yet, sprinkle one with salt and eat it with bread and a ripe tomato. Hard-cooked eggs are also great to take along on a picnic.

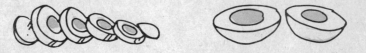

EGG SALAD

Here's what you need:

Bowl

Spatula

Egg slicer

Measuring cup

Tablespoon

Fork

4 Shelled, hard-cooked eggs

Onion flakes

MAYONNAISE

Mayonnaise

Pepper

Salt

MUSTARD

Prepared mustard

Here's what you do:

1 With the egg slicer, slice each egg across and lengthwise, and drop it into the bowl.

2 Add ¼ cup mayonnaise, 1 tablespoon mustard, and some onion flakes.

3 Mash everything together with a fork. If you like creamier egg salad, add more mayonnaise.

4 Add some salt, a little at a time, and pepper, until the egg salad tastes the way you like it. You might also add some chopped celery, green pepper, or carrot.

5 Cover the bowl, and put the egg salad into the refrigerator for at least an hour. The flavors will blend.

6 With a spatula, scrape all of the egg salad out of the bowl and serve it on a lettuce leaf.

Egg salad is also good for stuffing celery, stuffing tomatoes, and spreading on crackers. You can make it into a super sandwich with bacon, lettuce, and tomato. How about egg salad and sliced olives on crunchy, whole-wheat bread?

HONEY CORN NUTS

Note: If you are not allowed to use the oven or popcorn maker by yourself, ask a grownup for some help.

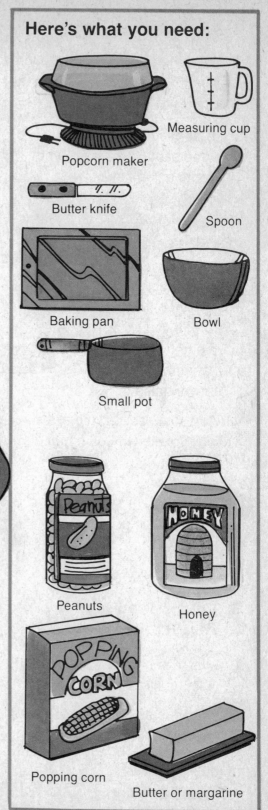

Here's what you need:

Popcorn maker

Measuring cup

Butter knife

Spoon

Baking pan

Bowl

Small pot

Peanuts

Honey

Popping corn

Butter or margarine

Here's what you do:

1 Preheat oven to 350°.

2 Use a popcorn-making machine to pop about 6 cups of popcorn (six cups *after* popping — not before).

3 Place ½ stick butter or margarine and ¼ cup honey in a small pot. Heat over a low heat until the margarine or butter is melted. Stir the mixture until it is blended.

4 Put the popcorn and ¾ cup shelled peanuts into a mixing bowl.

5 Pour the honey mixture over the popcorn and nuts, stirring to coat the popcorn evenly.

6 Pour the popcorn onto a baking pan. Spread it out to about 1 inch thick.

7 Bake for 10–15 minutes or until the Honey Corn Nuts are crisp.

8 Cool a bit and enjoy.

QUICK AND EASY CORN CHOWDER

Note: This recipe calls for use of the stove. If you are not allowed to use the stove alone, ask an adult for help.

Here's what you need:

Knife

Wooden spoon

Measuring spoons

Salt

Butter or margarine

Pepper

Cutting board

Can opener

Green pepper

Onion

Pot

Potholder

Can of creamed corn

Evaporated milk

Here's what you do:

1 Empty a large can of creamed corn into a pot.

2 Add 3 cups of evaporated milk, 1 tablespoon butter or margarine, 2 tablespoons diced onion, and 2 tablespoons chopped green pepper.

3 Add some salt and pepper.

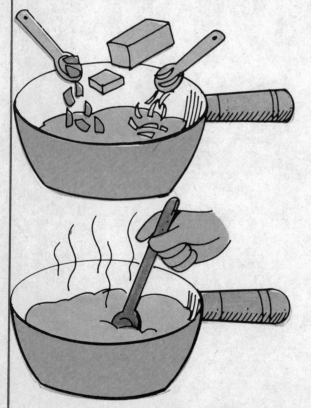

4 Carry the pot to the stove, and place it over a medium heat.

5 While the chowder is heating, stir it gently, with a wooden spoon.

6 Let the soup come to a boil, and then serve it piping hot. Serves 4–5 people.

Hint #1: If you like your chowder thicker, sprinkle a tablespoon or more of instant mashed potatoes into the pot.

Hint #2: Add a pinch of thyme for a real flavor treat!

This soup tastes wonderful on a cold, snowy day. Sit next to a window while you eat, and watch the falling snow.

CABBAGE SOUP FOR A CROWD!

Note: Ask an adult for help, if you are not allowed to use the stove by yourself.

Here's what you need:

Cutting board

Potholder

Measuring cup

Salt

Onion flakes

Caraway seeds

Lemon

Brown sugar

Large can tomato juice (46 oz.)

Measuring spoons

Can opener

Knife

Pepper

Head of cabbage

Celery

Carrots

Wooden spoon

Large covered pot

Water

Tomato puree

Here's what you do:

1   Pour the tomato juice, 2 cups water, and 2 cups tomato puree into a large pot.

2   Slice the cabbage into quarters. Remove the hard center core.

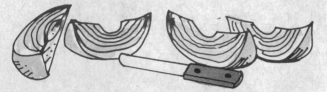

3   Cut each quarter into small pieces, and add them to the pot.

4   Chop 2 stalks of celery, including the leaves, and 2 carrots. Add them to the pot.

5   Add the juice from half a lemon, 1 tablespoon onion flakes, 1 tablespoon caraway seeds, 1 tablespoon sugar, 1 teaspoon salt, and some pepper.

6   Carry the pot to the stove, and place it on a medium-high heat. Stir with a wooden spoon.

7   When the soup starts to boil, turn the heat to low. Cover the pot and let the soup simmer (cook very gently) for 1 hour or until the vegetables are tender.

8   Peek in from time to time and stir the soup with your spoon. But always uncover the pot slowly. Let the steam escape away from you. *Remember to use a potholder!*

Hint: Float a spoonful of sour cream or yogurt in your soup. This soup is fun to make with other people. You can share the cutting and chopping. You can share the cleaning up. Then you can share the eating! If there is any soup left over, store it in the refrigerator. It tastes even better the next day.

HAMBURGER HEROES

Note: This recipe calls for use of the broiler. If you are not allowed to use the broiler alone, ask an adult for help.

Here's what you need:

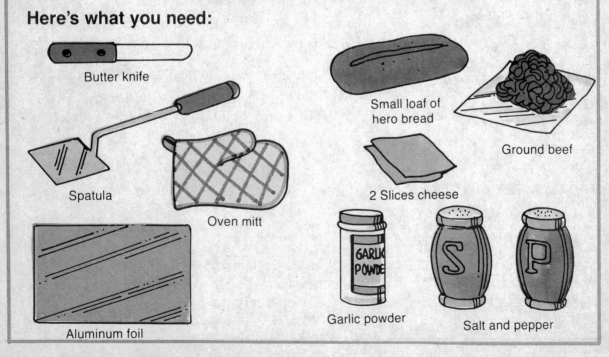

Butter knife

Spatula

Oven mitt

Aluminum foil

Small loaf of hero bread

Ground beef

2 Slices cheese

Garlic powder

Salt and pepper

Here's what you do:

1   Divide about 6 ounces of ground beef into two portions. Place the two portions on a sheet of aluminum foil.

2   Use a butter knife to flatten out the ground beef to about ¼ inch thick.

3   Place the sheet of foil in the center of the broiler rack and broil the meat on one side for 3 minutes. Then open the broiler and, with a spatula, flip the meat and broil 2 more minutes.

4   Cut the hero bread in half lengthwise.

5   Carefully open the broiler. Pull out the rack with a potholder. Use a spatula to lift a portion of meat onto each half of the bread.

6   Place a slice of cheese on each half. Broil the heroes until the cheese melts.

7   When they are done, place the hamburgers on a plate and serve.

TOSSED GREEN SALAD

Here's what you need:

Knife

Vegetable brush

Large fork and spoon

Plastic wrap

Cutting board

Salad bowl

Paper towels

Boston lettuce   Romaine lettuce   Iceberg lettuce

Cucumber   Spinach   Celery

Onion   Mushrooms

Cauliflower   Peppers   Tomatoes

Here's what you do:

1   Choose as many salad greens as you like, and wash them under cold, running water.

2   Pat them dry with paper towels.

3   Throw away any bruised or discolored greens and trim the spinach stems.

4   Tear the greens into bite-size pieces, and place them in the salad bowl.

5   Choose as many vegetables as you like and scrub them with a vegetable brush. Dry them with paper towels.

6   Cut them into slices, wedges, and chunks, and add them to the salad. Be very careful when doing any cutting.

7   Cover the bowl with plastic wrap, and refrigerate it until you are ready to serve.

8   At serving time, sprinkle the salad with dressing and toss.

Hint: Add cheese, ham, or turkey to your salad, and you have a complete meal. How about adding chunks of tuna fish and chopped, hard-cooked eggs?

Here's what you need:

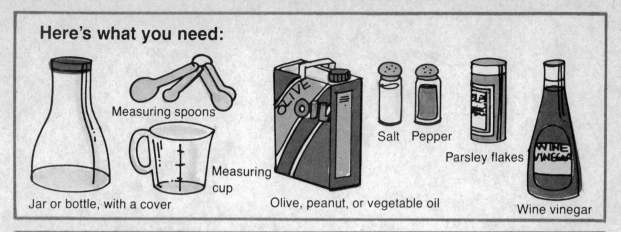

Jar or bottle, with a cover

Measuring spoons

Measuring cup

Olive, peanut, or vegetable oil

Salt Pepper

Parsley flakes

Wine vinegar

Here's what you do:

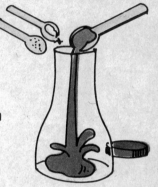

1 Combine 1 teaspoon salt, 1 teaspoon pepper, and 3 tablespoons wine vinegar in a jar.

2 Cover and shake the jar hard, so that the salt mixes with the vinegar.

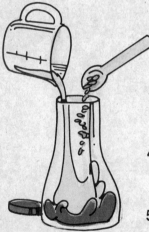

3 Add ¾ cup oil and 1 tablespoon parsley. Then shake the jar some more.

4 Now sprinkle as much dressing as you need on your salad.

5 Refrigerate the rest.

This is a basic salad dressing. To it, you can add a clove of crushed garlic or a pinch or two of herbs. How about adding tarragon, basil, or chervil? Try a tablespoon of chopped chives. Make your dressing extra fancy by adding ¼ cup of crumbled blue cheese!

QUICK AND EASY RUSSIAN DRESSING

Here's what you need:

Spoon

Measuring spoons

Wedge of lemon

Bowl

Measuring cup

Chili sauce or ketchup

Pickle relish

Mayonnaise

Here's what you do:

1. Combine ½ cup mayonnaise, 3 tablespoons chili sauce or ketchup, and 2 tablespoons pickle relish in a bowl.

2. Squeeze the juice from a lemon wedge into the bowl, and stir the mixture with a spoon until it is well blended. You may wish to add more pickle relish or chili sauce to suit your taste.

Russian dressing is perfect for spooning over lettuce chunks or hard-cooked eggs. It is delicious with cold chicken or turkey. Try it as a dip for raw vegetables.

CARROT SLAW

Here's what you need:

Grater

Wooden spoon

Mayonnaise

Raisins

Salt   Pepper

Bowl

Vegetable scraper

MAYONNAISE

3 Carrots

Lemon

Here's what you do:

1 With a vegetable scraper, scrape 3 carrots.

2 Using the coarse side of a grater, carefully grate the carrots over a mixing bowl.

3 Add a handful of raisins and enough mayonnaise to moisten the carrot slaw. Start with a little mayonnaise. Add more if you need it. Mix everything with a wooden spoon.

4 Add the juice from ½ lemon, a dash of salt, and some pepper. Mix again.

5 Chill the carrot slaw in the refrigerator for an hour or two.

FRUITY FRUIT PUNCH

Here's what you need:

Knife

Wooden spoon

Measuring cup

Can opener

Ice cubes

Strawberries

Pineapple chunks

2-Quart pitcher

Cutting board

Orange juice

Pink lemonade

Navel orange

Here's what you do:

1 Pour 2 cups orange juice and 2 cups pink lemonade into a pitcher.

2 Add a small can of pineapple chunks and the juice in which they are packed.

3 Add 1 cup strawberries to the pitcher, taking care to first cut any large strawberries in half.

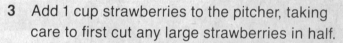

4 Peel a navel orange. Separate it into sections. Cut each section in thirds, and add them to the fruit punch.

5 Fill the pitcher with ice cubes.

6 Stir the punch with a wooden spoon until the pitcher is frosty.

Serve this fruit punch with straws and a spoon. Add some fresh mint leaves!

DANDY CANDY CHEWS

Here's what you need:

Bowl

Fork

Spoon

Plate

Measuring cup

Wax paper

½ Cup granola

¼ Cup raisins

½ Cup unsweetened coconut

¼ Cup honey

Here's what you do:

1 Put the granola, coconut, raisins, and honey into the mixing bowl.

2 Mix them together, with a fork, until they are well blended.

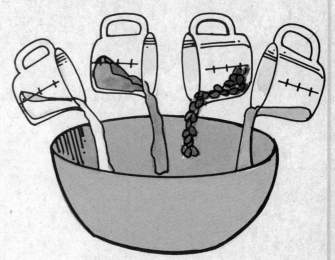

3 Chill the mixture in the refrigerator for 30 minutes. (Chilling makes it easier to handle.)

4 Cover a plate with a sheet of wax paper.

5 Take a spoonful of the candy mixture, and roll it into a small ball between your palms. *Hint:* Press the candy together, with your fingers, before rolling.

6 Place the candy ball on the wax paper.

7 Continue to make candy balls, until all of the mixture is used.

8 Chill the candies for about an hour.

9 Place them on a pretty plate, and serve.

These candies are packed with energy and are good for you. Wrap a few in wax paper, and pop them into your lunch box!

Measurements

If you should need to find out the metric values of measurements given in these recipes, this chart will help:

1 fluid ounce	=	30 milliliters
1 cup (8 oz.)	=	240 milliliters
1 pint	=	.47 liter
1 quart	=	.95 liter
1 gallon	=	3.8 liters
1 dry ounce	=	28 grams
1 pound	=	.45 kilogram
1 milliliter	=	.034 ounce
1 liter	=	2.1 pints
1 gram	=	.035 ounce
1 kilogram	=	2.2 pounds

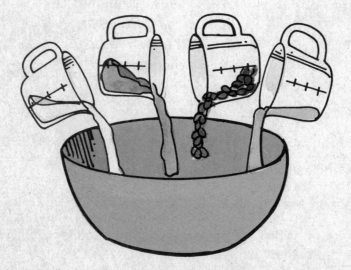